W9-BGW-542

FRAYSER

19.95

$19.95   FRA
CHILDREN
333.7
G479cm

DISCARDED BY
MEMPHIS PUBLIC LIBRARY

CONSERVATION-AREA
MAPS

Jack and Meg Gillett

PowerKiDS
press.

New York

Published in 2013 by The Rosen Publishing Group, Inc.
29 East 21st Street, New York, NY 10010

Copyright © 2013 Wayland/The Rosen Publishing Group, Inc.

All rights reserved. No part of this book may be reproduced in any form without permission in writing from the publisher, except by a reviewer.

Editor: Julia Adams
Designer: Rob Walster, Big Blu Design
Cover Design: Wayland
Map Art: Martin Sanders
Illustrations: Andy Stagg
Picture Research: Kathy Lockley/Julia Adams
Contributions by Richard and Louise Spilsbury

Picture Acknowledgments: All photography: Shutterstock, except: p. 8: Edwin Remsberg/ Alamy; p. 17, p. 18 (right): iStock Images; p. 18 (left): NASA/Goddard Space Flight Center Scientific Visualization Studio.

Library of Congress Cataloging-in-Publication Data

Gillett, Jack.
 Conservation-area maps / by Jack Gillett & Meg Gillett. — 1st ed.
    p. cm. — (Maps of the environmental world)
 Includes index.
 ISBN 978-1-4488-8611-1 (library binding) — ISBN 978-1-4488-8615-9 (pbk.) — ISBN 978-1-4488-8617-3 (6-pack)
 1. Natural areas—Juvenile literature. I. Gillett, Meg. II. Title.
 QH75.G55 2013
 333.7—dc23

                                    2012004332

Manufactured in the United States of America

CPSIA Compliance Information: Batch #B4S12PK: For Further Information contact Rosen Publishing, New York, New York at 1-800-237-9932

Contents

Introduction

Our planet and all the living things on it are under threat from people. We are harming many habitats and ecosystems through mining, drilling, fishing, and other activities in order to obtain the resources demanded by our growing population. We are mostly causing damaging pollution and global warming through using energy to power vehicles and generate electricity.

Conservation is the protection of wild places and living things. It is vital to protect global biodiversity to ensure species survive into the future, especially because some some species may become useful or valuable, for example to

Globe shows the location of the map region

Statistical feature for at-a-glance data

Pictures highlight features discussed or located on the map

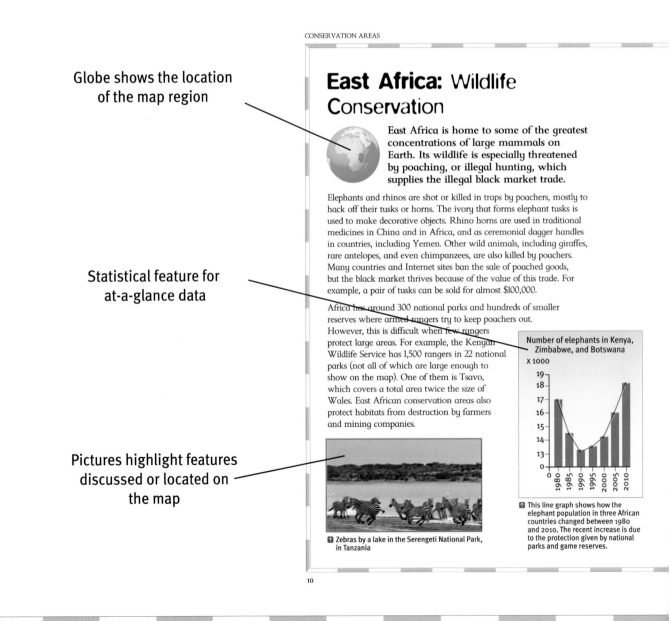

CONSERVATION AREAS

East Africa: Wildlife Conservation

East Africa is home to some of the greatest concentrations of large mammals on Earth. Its wildlife is especially threatened by poaching, or illegal hunting, which supplies the illegal black market trade.

Elephants and rhinos are shot or killed in traps by poachers, mostly to hack off their tusks or horns. The ivory that forms elephant tusks is used to make decorative objects. Rhino horns are used in traditional medicines in China and in Africa, and as ceremonial dagger handles in countries, including Yemen. Other wild animals, including giraffes, rare antelopes, and even chimpanzees, are also killed by poachers. Many countries and Internet sites ban the sale of poached goods, but the black market thrives because of the value of this trade. For example, a pair of tusks can be sold for almost $100,000.

Africa has around 300 national parks and hundreds of smaller reserves where armed rangers try to keep poachers out. However, this is difficult when few rangers protect large areas. For example, the Kenyan Wildlife Service has 1,500 rangers in 22 national parks (not all of which are large enough to show on the map). One of them is Tsavo, which covers a total area twice the size of Wales. East African conservation areas also protect habitats from destruction by farmers and mining companies.

Number of elephants in Kenya, Zimbabwe, and Botswana
x 1000

19
18
17
16
15
14
13
0

1980 1985 1990 1995 2000 2005 2010

This line graph shows how the elephant population in three African countries changed between 1980 and 2010. The recent increase is due to the protection given by national parks and game reserves.

Zebras by a lake in the Serengeti National Park, in Tanzania

10

improve human health. It is impossible to conserve all places on Earth, but there are many conservation areas. Some protect large regions and others protect just a few rare species.

This book looks at the location and variety of conservation areas, the wildlife and places they seek to protect, and the challenges to and successes of the conservation measures put in place to protect them. It also locates areas that are threatened or will become threatened in the near future and that are in need of conservation measures.

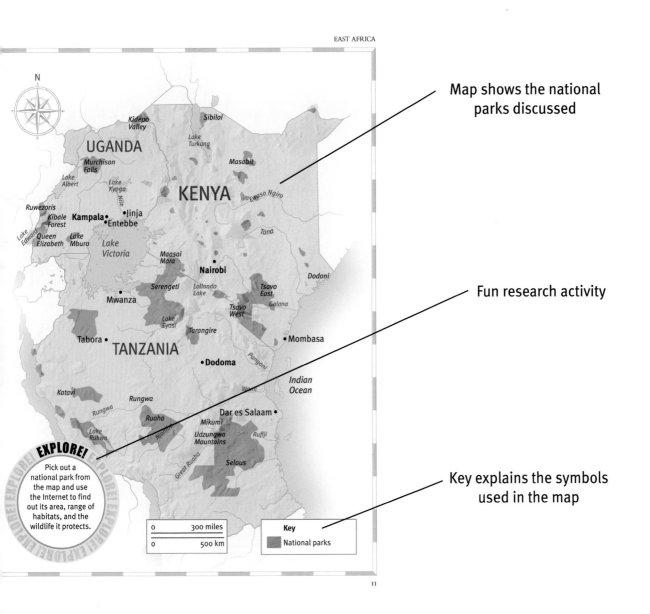

EAST AFRICA

Map shows the national parks discussed

Fun research activity

Key explains the symbols used in the map

EXPLORE!

Pick out a national park from the map and use the Internet to find out its area, range of habitats, and the wildlife it protects.

11

5

South America:
Sustainable Forestry

Trees are vital to life on Earth because they absorb carbon dioxide from the air and replace it with oxygen. But trees are being cut down, especially in tropical rain forests.

Warm, humid tropical rain forest is home to almost 70 percent of all species. Much is located in South America, but under threat because trees are being cut down faster than they are being replanted. Deforestation here is driven by demand for timber and wood products, including plywood and paper. The cleared land is also used to raise cattle for beef and as a source for valuable oil. These activities are important to the economic development of less developed countries such as Brazil because they generate income to invest in new roads, hospitals, and other infrastructure.

South American governments completely protect some areas of forest, such as the Juruena National Park, in Brazil, to stop deforestation. But as the rain forest is so enormous and economically important, they also manage areas of forest sustainably. Sustainable forestry controls deforestation and replants land with native species to maintain biodiversity and forest size. It conserves the shared forest resource into the future for people and wildlife. In Bolivia, the deforestation rate is actually slower in sustainably managed forest than in protected areas.

⬆ The Iguazú Falls are shared by the Iguazú National Park (Argentina) and Iguaçú National Park (Brazil). These parks are UNESCO World Heritage sites.

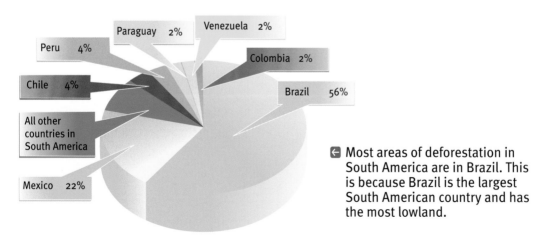

- Paraguay 2%
- Venezuela 2%
- Peru 4%
- Colombia 2%
- Chile 4%
- Brazil 56%
- All other countries in South America
- Mexico 22%

⬅ Most areas of deforestation in South America are in Brazil. This is because Brazil is the largest South American country and has the most lowland.

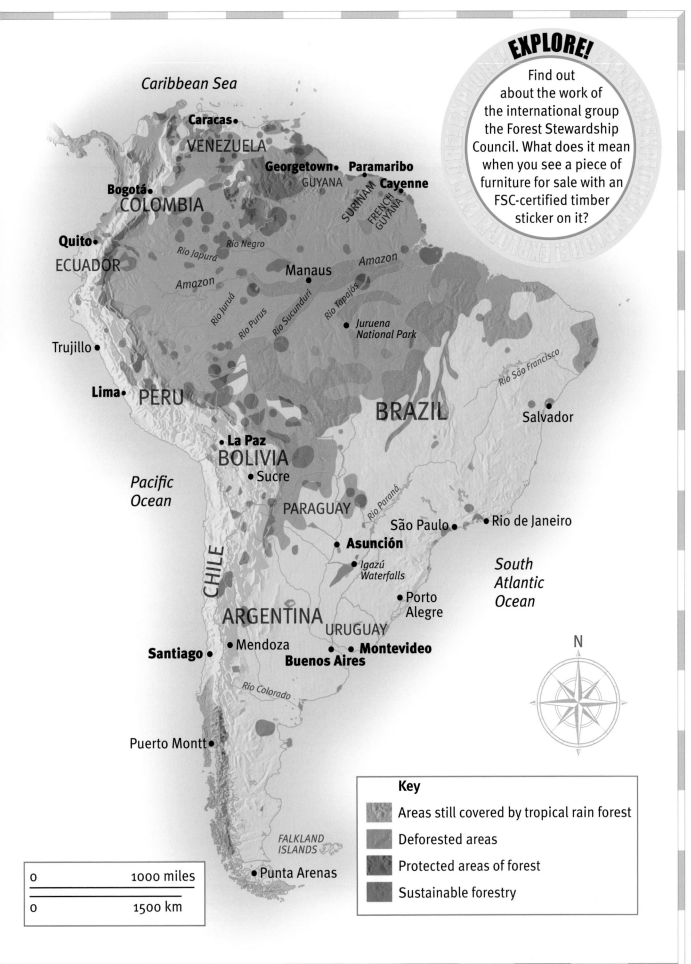

Caribbean Sea

Caracas•

VENEZUELA

Georgetown•   Paramaribo•
GUYANA   SURINAM Cayenne•
                      FRENCH
Bogotá•   GUYANA
COLOMBIA

Quito•   Rio Negro

ECUADOR   Rio Japurá   Amazon
                                        Amazon
              Amazon   Manaus•
Rio Juruá
                    Rio Purus Rio Sucunduri Rio Tapajós
Trujillo•
                              Juruena
                              National Park

Lima• PERU
                                              Rio São Francisco

                              BRAZIL
                                        Salvador•

La Paz•
BOLIVIA
    •Sucre

Pacific
Ocean
              PARAGUAY   Rio Paraná
                              São Paulo• •Rio de Janeiro

              Asunción•

CHILE   •Igazú   South
              Waterfalls   Atlantic
                              Ocean
              Porto
ARGENTINA   Alegre•
    URUGUAY
Santiago• •Mendoza • •Montevideo
        Buenos Aires

              Rio Colorado

Puerto Montt•   N

FALKLAND
ISLANDS

0   1000 miles
0   1500 km

•Punta Arenas

EXPLORE!
Find out about the work of the international group the Forest Stewardship Council. What does it mean when you see a piece of furniture for sale with an FSC-certified timber sticker on it?

Key

Areas still covered by tropical rain forest

Deforested areas

Protected areas of forest

Sustainable forestry

United States: Saving the Soil

Parts of the western United States have large areas of dry land and desert, including the Mojave and Sonoran. They are caused by the land being in the rain shadow of mountain ranges, including the Sierra Nevada.

Many of the drier areas in the western United States are in danger of desertification. This is when land dries out or becomes damaged, so the soil crumbles to dust. Wind-blown dust chokes water channels and blows onto settlements and farmland. Scientists predict that the remaining dry grasslands in the US west are threatened by desertification because of higher temperatures. This is a result of global warming and droughts caused by changing weather patterns.

One of the worst cases of desertification in history happened in the United States in the 1930s, in an area called the dust bowl. Soil turned to giant dust clouds because of land damage through ploughing and several years of drought. Thousands of farming families had to leave the area. Farming in the region recovered when it started raining again, but it relies on irrigation from underground water supplies that are reducing every year.

EXPLORE!

The Atacama Desert can't spread outward to the west or the east. Discover why not.

In the southwestern United States, people are trying to prevent desertification in different ways. For example, farmers plant trees or build fences to trap blown soil. They improve the soil condition by planting deep-rooted crops and leaving crop remains in fields after harvest, so roots hold onto soil.

⬅ US farmers use a relatively new technique called no-till when planting new seed. Instead of ploughing the soil, machines create a thin slit for the seeds, which means the top soil remains undisturbed and covered by crop remains. This protects soil from erosion.

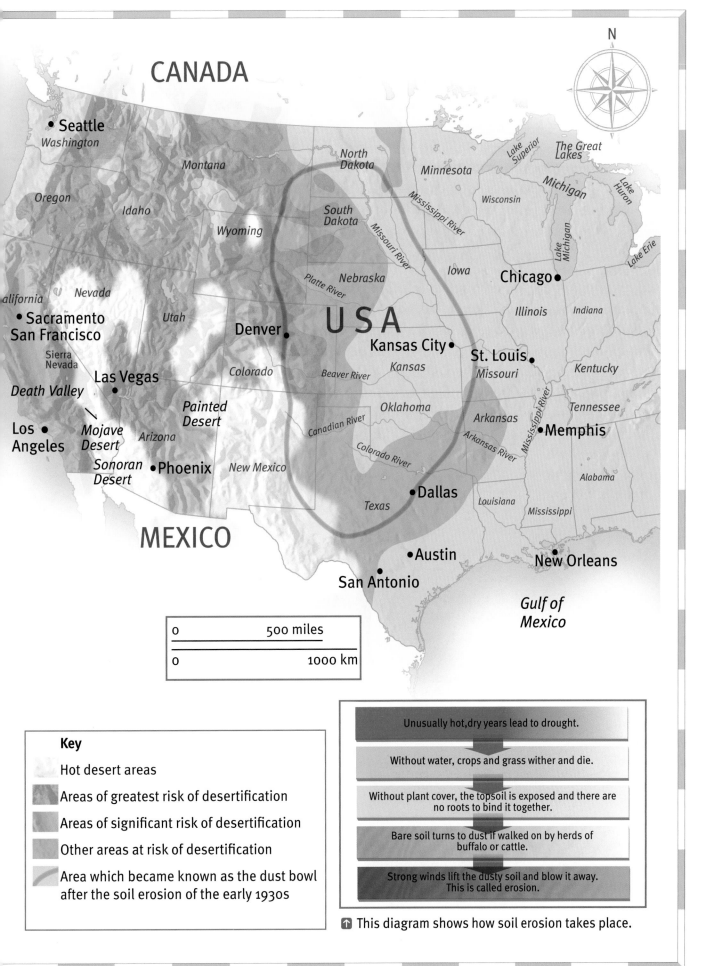

N

CANADA

Seattle
Washington

Montana

Oregon

Idaho

Wyoming

North
Dakota

South
Dakota

Missouri River

Minnesota

Mississippi River

Wisconsin

Lake
Superior

The Great
Lakes

Michigan

Lake
Huron

Lake
Michigan

Lake
Erie

California

Nevada

Utah

Colorado

Platte River

Nebraska

Iowa

U S A

Illinois

Indiana

Sacramento
San Francisco

Denver

Kansas City

St. Louis

Kentucky

Sierra
Nevada

Beaver River

Kansas

Missouri

Las Vegas

Death Valley

Painted
Desert

Colorado

Oklahoma

Canadian River

Arkansas

Arkansas River

Tennessee

Mississippi River

Memphis

Los
Angeles

Mojave
Desert

Arizona

Colorado River

Sonoran
Desert

Phoenix

New Mexico

Alabama

Dallas

Louisiana

Mississippi

MEXICO

Texas

Austin

New Orleans

San Antonio

Gulf of
Mexico

0	500 miles
0	1000 km

Key

Hot desert areas

Areas of greatest risk of desertification

Areas of significant risk of desertification

Other areas at risk of desertification

Area which became known as the dust bowl after the soil erosion of the early 1930s

Unusually hot, dry years lead to drought.
Without water, crops and grass wither and die.
Without plant cover, the topsoil is exposed and there are no roots to bind it together.
Bare soil turns to dust if walked on by herds of buffalo or cattle.
Strong winds lift the dusty soil and blow it away. This is called erosion.

⬆ This diagram shows how soil erosion takes place.

East Africa: Wildlife Conservation

East Africa is home to some of the greatest concentrations of large mammals on Earth. Its wildlife is especially threatened by poaching, or illegal hunting, which supplies the illegal black market trade.

Elephants and rhinos are shot or killed in traps by poachers, mostly to hack off their tusks or horns. The ivory that forms elephant tusks is used to make decorative objects. Rhino horns are used in traditional medicines in China and in Africa, and as ceremonial dagger handles in countries, including Yemen. Other wild animals, including giraffes, rare antelopes, and even chimpanzees, are also killed by poachers. Many countries and Internet sites ban the sale of poached goods, but the black market thrives because of the value of this trade. For example, a pair of tusks can be sold for almost $100,000.

Africa has around 300 national parks and hundreds of smaller reserves where armed rangers try to keep poachers out. However, this is difficult when few rangers protect large areas. For example, the Kenyan Wildlife Service has 1,500 rangers in 22 national parks (not all of which are large enough to show on the map). One of them is Tsavo, which covers a total area twice the size of Wales. East African conservation areas also protect habitats from destruction by farmers and mining companies.

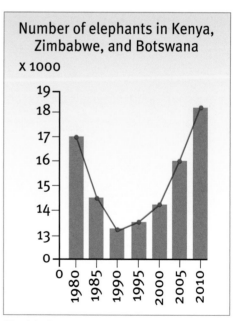

Number of elephants in Kenya, Zimbabwe, and Botswana

X 1000

⬆ This line graph shows how the elephant population in three African countries changed between 1980 and 2010. The recent increase is due to the protection given by national parks and game reserves.

⬆ Zebras by a lake in the Serengeti National Park, in Tanzania

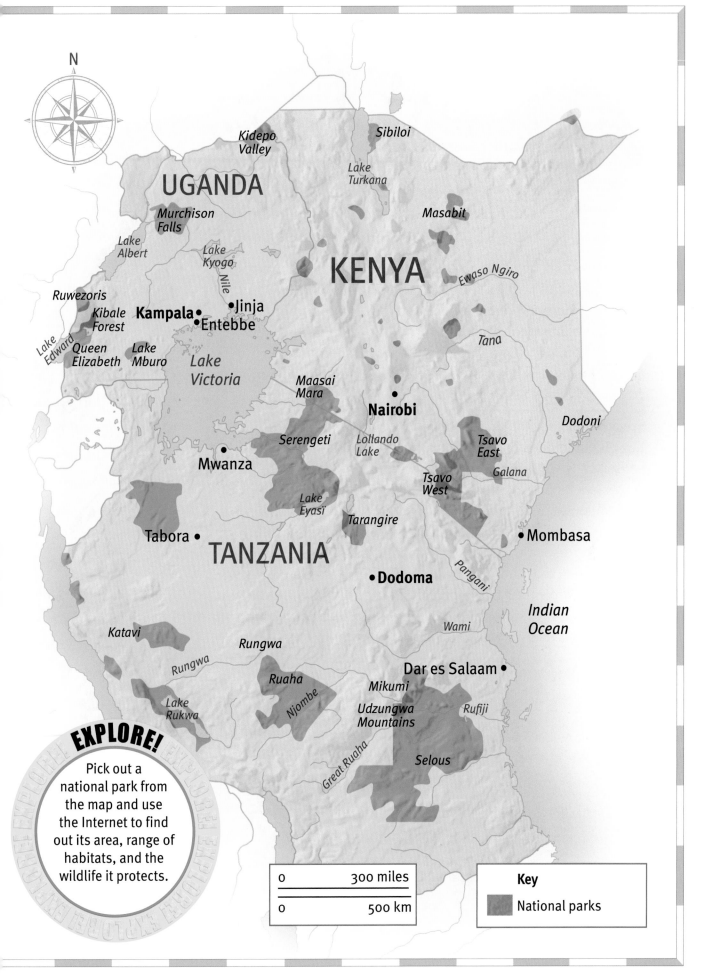

N

Kidepo
Valley

Sibiloi

UGANDA

Lake
Turkana

Murchison
Falls

Masabit

Lake
Albert

Lake
Kyogo

KENYA

Ewaso Ngiro

Nile

Ruwezoris

Kibale
Forest

Kampala •

• Jinja

• Entebbe

Tana

Lake
Edward

Queen
Elizabeth

Lake
Mburo

Lake
Victoria

Maasai
Mara

• Nairobi

Serengeti

Lollando
Lake

Tsavo
East

Dodoni

Mwanza •

Galana

Tsavo
West

Lake
Eyasï

Tarangire

Tabora •

• Mombasa

TANZANIA

Pangani

• Dodoma

Katavi

Rungwa

Wami

Indian
Ocean

Rungwa

Ruaha

Dar es Salaam •

Mikumi

Lake
Rukwa

Njombe

Udzungwa
Mountains

Rufiji

Great Ruaha

Selous

EXPLORE!

Pick out a
national park from
the map and use
the Internet to find
out its area, range of
habitats, and the
wildlife it protects.

0	300 miles
0	500 km

Key

National parks

Asia: Species Conservation

Asia's human population is the fastest-growing on the planet and this puts great pressure on wildlife habitats. As a result, its native tigers and apes, such as the orangutan, are among the "top 10" of endangered species.

Habitat loss is one of the largest threats to species around the world. This can happen for many reasons, but all are due to growth of human population, such as the expansion of cities and deforestation for timber or farmland. For example, the giant panda, which eats almost nothing but bamboo, became endangered when bamboo forests were cleared to grow more crops for China's rising population.

Species that are globally in danger are put on the IUCN Red List of Threatened Species. This identifies species requiring conservation in order to avoid the risk of extinction. Many of Asia's species are on the list, including orangutans in Indonesia and Malaysia, and tigers throughout the region. Today there are fewer than 3,000 tigers in Asia. This is because of poaching for body parts, use in traditional medicines, and because the forest habitats they live and hunt in have been extensively cut down over the last century. Some tigers are protected in conservation areas, including 39 Project Tiger reserves in India, but in many parts of Asia tigers have little protection.

EXPLORE!

Make a list of 10 critically endangered Asian species from the Red List by visiting the website www.iucnredlist.org .

 A young orangutan in Borneo's Sepilok Forest Reserve

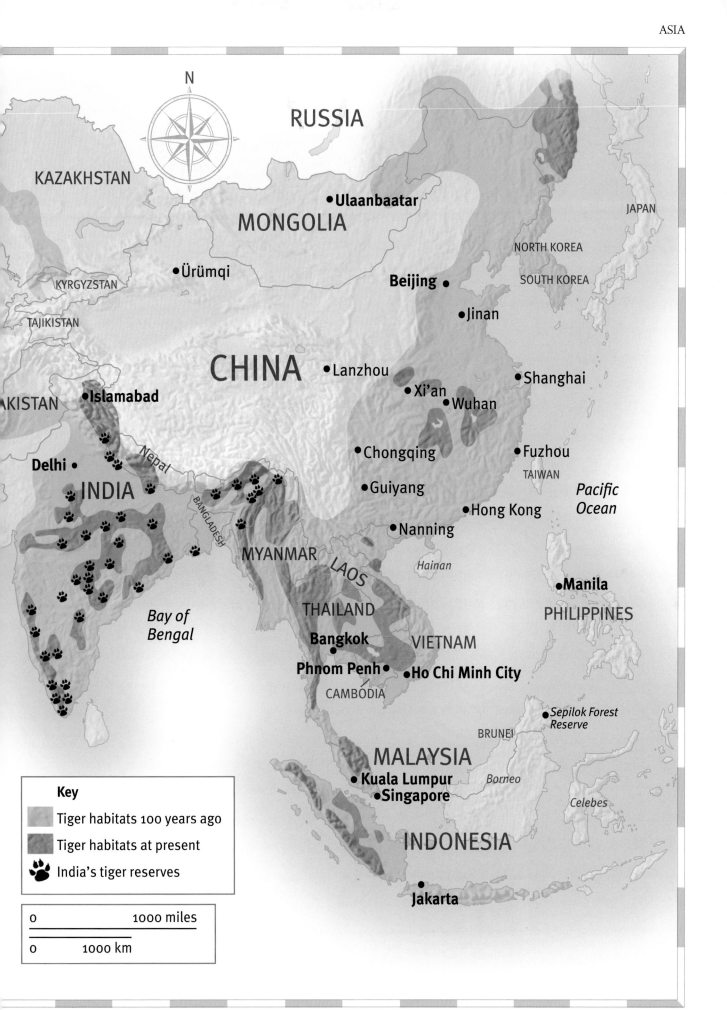

N

RUSSIA

KAZAKHSTAN

•**Ulaanbaatar**

MONGOLIA

•Ürümqi

KYRGYZSTAN

Beijing •

NORTH KOREA

SOUTH KOREA

JAPAN

TAJIKISTAN

•Jinan

CHINA

•Lanzhou

•Shanghai

•Xi'an

•Wuhan

KISTAN

•**Islamabad**

Nepal

Delhi •

BANGLADESH

INDIA

•Chongqing

•Fuzhou

TAIWAN

•Guiyang

•Nanning

Pacific
Ocean

•Hong Kong

MYANMAR

LAOS

Hainan

Bay of
Bengal

THAILAND

•**Manila**

PHILIPPINES

VIETNAM

Bangkok

Phnom Penh •

•**Ho Chi Minh City**

CAMBODIA

Sepilok Forest
Reserve

BRUNEI

MALAYSIA

Borneo

•**Kuala Lumpur**

•**Singapore**

Celebes

INDONESIA

Jakarta

Key

Tiger habitats 100 years ago

Tiger habitats at present

India's tiger reserves

| 0 | 1000 miles |
| 0 | 1000 km |

Europe: Wetland Conservation

Wetlands are ecosystems, such as bogs and swamps, where the soil is saturated with water for all or most of the year. They are very important ecosystems as they hold water and control flooding.

Europe's wetlands are under threat. Since 1900, around 60 percent of the original area of Europe's wetlands has disappeared. This is a result of draining to create farmland, build new homes on, and extract freshwater for the growing population. Smaller wetlands not only have fewer habitats for wildlife, but also store less freshwater that humans and other animals need. Recreational use, such as boating and fishing, disturbs water birds and other wetland animals, especially during their breeding seasons. This means that their numbers are falling. Wetlands are also polluted by agricultural and industrial chemicals washed off the land. This impacts the wildlife and water plants, too. One in three European freshwater fish species are threatened because of changes to wetlands.

Conserving existing wetlands is now a high environmental priority across Europe. Some are conserved in national parks and reserves. For example, in the UK, the Wildfowl and Wetlands Trust runs reserves where it plants new reed-bed habitats, keeps lakes at a constant depth, and makes sure the water is clean so water birds can breed.

⬆ Martin Mere is one of the Wildfowl and Wetlands Trust's sites. It is also a favorite stopping-off point for migrating geese and swans.

PORTUGAL

Delta of the River Guadalquiver

⬅ The Camargue Regional Park, in southern France, is one of Europe's largest wetlands. This protected area is famous for its wild horses and colorful flamingos.

EXPLORE!

Find out about the Ramsar Convention and its importance for wetland ecosystem conservation worldwide.

Key

Wetland reserve

Wetland

ICELAND

Arctic Ocean

N

SWEDEN

NORWAY

FINLAND

• Stockholm

ESTONIA

Estonia Marshes

LATVIA

Scotland

Northern Ireland

UNITED KINGDOM

North Sea

DENMARK

Baltic Sea

LITHUANIA

RUSS. FED.

Ireland

Martin Mere Wetland Centre

The Fens

England

Wales

NETHERLANDS

BELARUS

London •

• Berlin

BELGIUM

GERMANY

POLAND

Kiev •

Paris •

Poitevin Marsh

CZECH REPUBLIC

SLOVAKIA

UKRAINE

FRANCE

SWITZERLAND

AUSTRIA

HUNGARY

MOLDOVA

Alps

Alps

SLOVENIA

ROMANIA

Delta of the River Danube

CROATIA

The Camargue

Pyrenees

ANDORRA

SAN MARINO

BOSNIA AND HERZEGOVINA

drid

SPAIN

ITALY

Mostar Marshes

SERBIA

BULGARIA

Black Sea

Corsica

VATICAN CITY

• Rome

MONTENEGRO

Sardinia

MACEDONIA

ALBANIA

Mediterranean Sea

GREECE

Sicily

•Athens

MALTA

| 0 | 500 miles |
| 0 | 1000 km |

New Zealand: Marine Conservation

Oceans and seas cover two-thirds of our planet. They are complex ecosystems that are rich in wildlife, but increasingly endangered due to human activities.

Many marine species are endangered. Some are harmed by pollution, such as when oil, industrial chemicals, or garbage are spilled or dumped into the ocean. Enormous nets catching anything in their path can destroy whole populations of fish.

New Zealand is a pioneer in marine conservation with over 30 marine reserves. The map shows where they are located. The first ever marine reserve, around Goat Island, was created in 1975 and transformed the overfished waters into a richly biodiverse area. It is a "no-take" reserve, which means all fishing is banned. Tourist divers are welcome to swim and look, but never kill or otherwise disturb wildlife. There are no barriers around the reserve, but conservation rangers patrol the area. In other countries marine parks, sanctuaries, and reserves provide different levels of conservation. For example, fishing, dredging, and other activities are allowed, but strictly controlled in many US marine sanctuaries.

EXPLORE!

Find out about the species and marine landscape conserved at two different marine reserves using the interactive map at www. doc.govt.nz/conservation/ marine-and-coastal/marine-protected-areas/marine-reserves-a-z/.

Around 12 percent of land is protected, but under 0.5 percent of oceans and seas are. The pressure is growing to catch more fish and find more oil under sea beds. However, more countries are conserving their waters. For example, in October 2010 the UK established the largest no-take marine protected area in the world in the Chagos Archipelago, in the Indian ocean.

⬆ These snappers are at the Poor Knights Island marine reserve. The number of snappers in this reserve has increased rapidly since its no-take status was introduced.

N

Poor Knights Island

Whangarei Harbour
Goat Island

Long Bay   Te Matuku Bay

Auckland

Te Whanganui a Hei
Tuhua

Volkner Rocks

**North
Island**

Parininihi

Tapuae

Te Tapuwae o
Rongokako

Tasman Sea

Te Angiangi

Tonga Island   Kapiti

Westhaven   Horoirangi

**NEW
ZEALAND**

Long Island

Wellington

Taputeranga

Christchurch

Flea Bay

Sutherland
Sound   Milford Sound

Gold Arm   **South
Island**

Gaer Arm

The Gut

Elizabeth 1

Wet Jacket
Arm

Five finger
peninsular

Long Sound

*South
Pacific
Ocean*

• **Dunedin**

Ulva Island

0	100 miles
0	200 km

Key

▨ Marine mammal sanctuary

🚫 No fishing/no-take area

Antarctica: Fragile Environments

Antarctica is the permanently ice-covered continent around the South Pole. It has the coldest, windiest climate on Earth and is surrounded by the freezing, rough Southern Ocean.

Few life forms can survive on Antarctic land other than lichens, although penguins breed there in the slightly warmer summer. However, vast numbers of microscopic phytoplankton grow in the mineral-rich waters, supporting the Antarctic food web. Phytoplankton are eaten by shrimplike animals called krill. Krill are the main food not only for fish eaten by penguins and seabirds, but also for the enormous blue, fin, and sei whales.

Global warming is raising the temperature of the Southern Ocean and shrinking its sea ice. Krill numbers are falling because there are fewer phytoplankton, which flourish best under sea ice and in colder water. Illegal overfishing is also a problem. There are fewer whales because there are fewer krill, but also because of illegal whaling. This is despite the Southern Ocean Whale Sanctuary, an area where whaling is banned.

Antarctica was harmed by waste from scientific stations before the dumping of waste was banned under the international Antarctic Treaty in 1959. (The map shows the scientific stations and which countries they belong to.) However, global demand for the abundant minerals hidden under the ice, and oil discovered deep in the South Atlantic, may threaten Antarctica in the future.

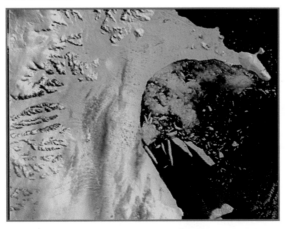

⬆ Parts of the Antarctic ice shelf are retreating further every year due to global warming. This image shows a 500 square mile (800 km²) ice shelf collapsing into the Weddell Sea.

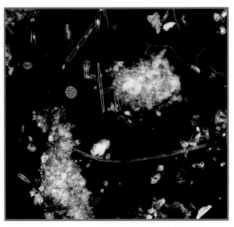

⬆ Microscopic phytoplankton are essential to the whole Antarctic food web.

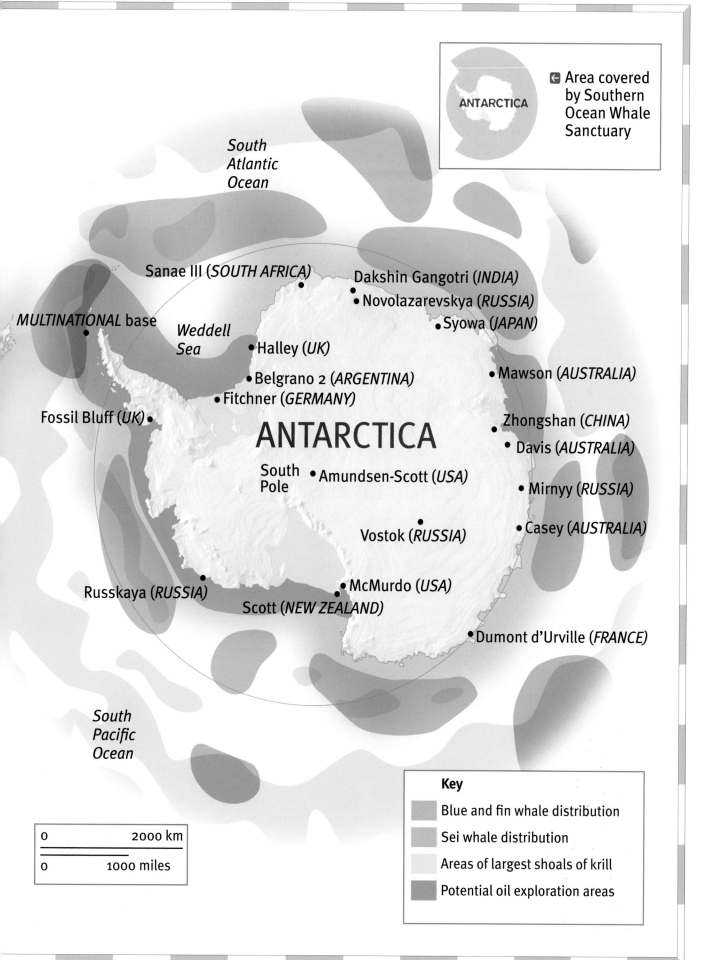

South Atlantic Ocean

Sanae III (*SOUTH AFRICA*)

Dakshin Gangotri (*INDIA*)

Novolazarevskya (*RUSSIA*)

Syowa (*JAPAN*)

MULTINATIONAL base

Weddell Sea

Halley (*UK*)

Mawson (*AUSTRALIA*)

Belgrano 2 (*ARGENTINA*)

Fitchner (*GERMANY*)

Fossil Bluff (*UK*)

ANTARCTICA

Zhongshan (*CHINA*)

Davis (*AUSTRALIA*)

South Pole

Amundsen-Scott (*USA*)

Mirnyy (*RUSSIA*)

Vostok (*RUSSIA*)

Casey (*AUSTRALIA*)

Russkaya (*RUSSIA*)

McMurdo (*USA*)

Scott (*NEW ZEALAND*)

Dumont d'Urville (*FRANCE*)

South Pacific Ocean

0	2000 km
0	1000 miles

Key

Blue and fin whale distribution

Sei whale distribution

Areas of largest shoals of krill

Potential oil exploration areas

Australia: Coral Reefs

Coral reefs are often called "the rain forests of the sea" because they are the habitat for an extraordinary range of wildlife. The 1,250-mile-(2,012 km) long Great Barrier Reef, in Australia, is the world's largest reef system.

Reefs are formed by tiny marine animals, called coral polyps, that live in big colonies. Polyps secrete protective mineral skeletons around their bodies, so rocklike reefs gradually form over many years. Polyps survive because tiny algae inside their bodies make food using sunlight. Coral needs warm, clear water with enough minerals to make skeletons.

One in ten reefs globally have been destroyed by people, such as fishermen using dynamite to catch fish. Reefs are damaged when tourists walk on coral and break off pieces as souvenirs. Corals are sensitive to global warming. For example, coral dies and turns white (bleaches) in warmer water because algae in polyps die.

The Great Barrier Reef is a UNESCO World Heritage area. This recognizes the natural, cultural, and economic importance of the reef and encourages tourism. There is also a larger marine park run by the Australian government to conserve the reef. Park maps are color zoned. No one can enter pink zones without official permission, but tourists can boat and dive in light-blue zones.

EXPLORE!

Visit www.reefed.edu.au/home/explorer/animals/marine_invertebrates/echinoderms/crown_of_thorns to investigate a major natural threat to corals making up the Great Barrier Reef.

⬆ When corals die, a whole habitat disappears with them. Areas of dead coral in the Great Barrier Reef are deserted of marine wildlife.

⬆ Conservation measures have been very successful in recovering some of the badly affected areas of the Great Barrier Reef.

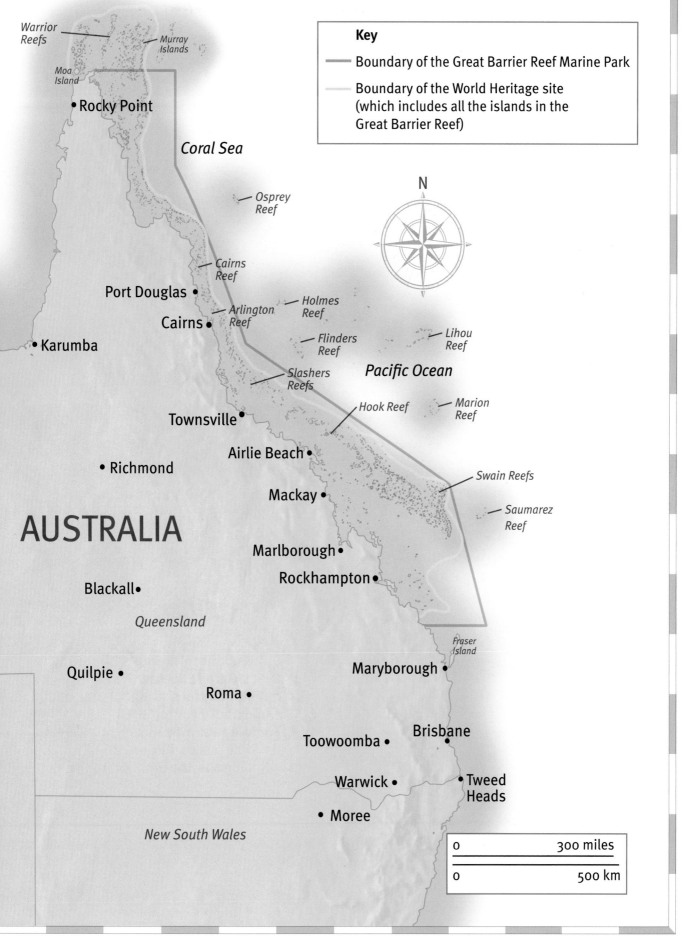

Warrior
Reefs
Murray
Islands
Moa
Island
● Rocky Point
Coral Sea
*Osprey
Reef*

Key
— Boundary of the Great Barrier Reef Marine Park
— Boundary of the World Heritage site
(which includes all the islands in the
Great Barrier Reef)

N

*Cairns
Reef*
Port Douglas ●
*Arlington
Reef*
Cairns ●
*Holmes
Reef*
● Karumba
*Flinders
Reef*
*Lihou
Reef*
*Slashers
Reefs*
Pacific Ocean
Townsville ●
Hook Reef
*Marion
Reef*
Airlie Beach ●
● Richmond
Swain Reefs
Mackay ●
*Saumarez
Reef*

AUSTRALIA

Marlborough ●
Rockhampton ●
Blackall ●
Queensland
*Fraser
Island*
Quilpie ●
Maryborough ●
Roma ●
Brisbane
Toowoomba ● ●
Warwick ● ● Tweed
Heads
● Moree
New South Wales

0		300 miles
0		500 km

The World: Whaling

In the past 200 years, populations of many whale species have been in decline all over the world. This is due to large-scale commercial whaling.

Whales have been hunted for the past 10,000 years by tribes, such as the Inuit people, in polar regions. They hunted whales for meat, blubber for fuel, and baleen for rope. Commercial whaling started during the Industrial Revolution with demand for products such as whale oil to lubricate machines. Whale populations plummeted once explosive harpoons were invented that could kill whales from a distance, and powerful ships could follow whale migrations and process many dead whales.

The humpback whale feeds on krill in polar waters in summer and breeds in tropical waters in winter. For years, whalers from Russia, the United States, and Japan hunted during summer in the North Pacific. During the 20th century the global whale population dropped nearly 90 percent. The International Whaling Commission banned commercial humpback whaling in 1966 to avoid the extinction of the species.

As whales range over such large areas, bans are almost impossible to enforce. Some countries, including Japan, carry on whaling other species for scientific and cultural reasons. Today there are around 60,000 humpbacks and the population is rising, but they still face threats, including pollution and collisions with ships.

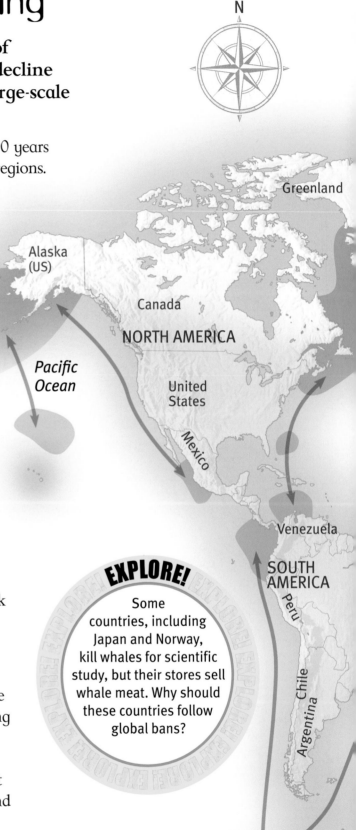

EXPLORE!

Some countries, including Japan and Norway, kill whales for scientific study, but their stores sell whale meat. Why should these countries follow global bans?

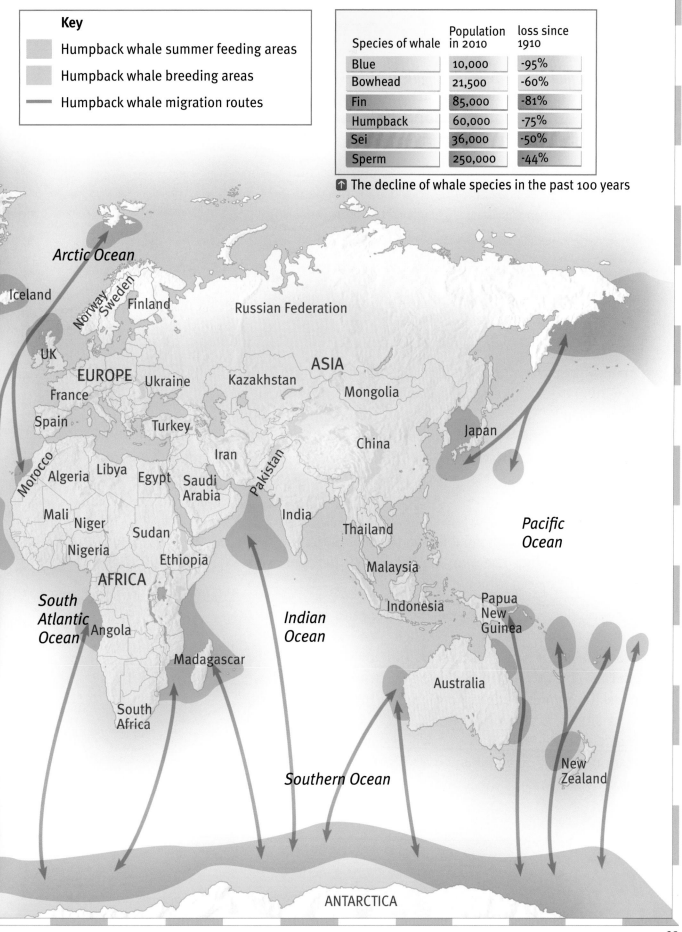

Key

Humpback whale summer feeding areas

Humpback whale breeding areas

Humpback whale migration routes

Species of whale	Population in 2010	loss since 1910
Blue	10,000	-95%
Bowhead	21,500	-60%
Fin	85,000	-81%
Humpback	60,000	-75%
Sei	36,000	-50%
Sperm	250,000	-44%

⬆ The decline of whale species in the past 100 years

Arctic Ocean

Iceland

Norway Sweden Finland

Russian Federation

UK

EUROPE Ukraine Kazakhstan ASIA

France Mongolia

Spain Turkey China Japan

Morocco Iran Pakistan

Algeria Libya Egypt Saudi Arabia

Mali Niger Sudan India Thailand Pacific Ocean

Nigeria Ethiopia Malaysia

AFRICA Papua New Guinea

South Atlantic Ocean Angola Indonesia

Indian Ocean

Madagascar Australia

South Africa

Southern Ocean New Zealand

ANTARCTICA

The World: Overfishing

Fishing is one of the world's most important food industries. It employs about 250 million people globally and supplies around 100 million tons (91 million t) of fish per year.

Fish is an important protein source for humans, and as the world population is increasing, so too does the demand for food. The fishing industry is meeting this demand with more efficient fishing boats. They have onboard refrigerators to store the catch and sonar systems to locate fish shoals. However, in certain areas more fish are caught than can be replenished naturally. This is called overfishing.

About 75 percent of marine fish stocks are now fully exploited or seriously depleted. These include Atlantic cod, Mediterranean/Atlantic tuna and swordfish, and Chilean sea bass. Overfishing is sometimes the result of high demand for certain fish. For example, tuna caught globally is in demand from Japan because many people there eat it raw as sushi. The bluefin tuna is now one of the most endangered fish in the world, mainly due to overfishing. The map shows which other species are being overfished in which areas.

Conservation measures for threatened species include quotas limiting the total weight of fish each boat can catch in a year. They also require the use of large-mesh nets that allow smaller, younger fish to escape, so they may grow and breed. International groups such as the Marine Stewardship Council help conserve threatened fish species by encouraging supermarkets to label fish that where caught sustainably, so consumers can avoid buying overfished species.

Greenla

Alaska (US)

Canada

Herring

NORTH AMERICA

Grand Banks

Salmon

USA

Lobs

Mexico

Shrimp

Tuna

Venez

SOUTH AMERIC

Herring

Peru

Sardines

Chile

Argentina

EXPLORE!

Visit http://
www.ifrfish.org/
wildfish-coalition to
find out how fish
farming can harm wild
marine species.

Arctic Ocean

Cod

Cod

Herring

Haddock

Cod

Norway

Sweden

Finland

Russia

North
Sea

Baltic Sea

ASIA

Pollack

Squid

UK

Mackerel

EUROPE

France

Ukraine

Kazakhstan

Mongolia

China

Shrimp

Sea of
Japan

Japan

Spain

Tuna

Turkey

Sardines

Mediterranean Sea

Iran

Pakistan

India

East
China
Sea

Morocco

Egypt

Saudi
Arabia

Shrimp

Pacific
Ocean

Mali

Niger

Sudan

Sardines

Thailand

Shrimp

Nigeria

Ethiopia

AFRICA

Tuna

Malaysia

Indonesia

Papua
New
Guinea

Atlantic
Ocean

Indian Ocean

Java Sea

Angola

Madagascar

Australia

South
Africa

Anchovy

Lobster

Cape of
Good Hope

Lobster

New
Zealand

Key

Main fishing areas

0   2500 miles

0   5000 km

Southern Ocean

ANTARCTICA

25

Europe: Air Pollution

Air pollution is when gases and particles make the atmosphere dirty and harm living things. One of the areas where air pollution is very widespread is Western Europe.

Most air pollution in Europe is caused by burning fossil fuels in vehicles, power stations, and factories to generate energy. This releases gases, such as ozone, and tiny specks of partly burned fuel. When the gases dissolve in tiny droplets of water, they form acid rain. This rain kills trees because it stops them from taking in vital nutrients. It also pollutes lakes, harms freshwater animals, and damages buildings by dissolving stone. Smog is a dangerous form of air pollution made when ozone and tiny specks of burned fuel (called particulates) react with sunlight. Smog causes breathing problems for people in some cities, including Rome and Moscow.

Across Europe, many cities have Low Emission Zones (LEZs) – areas where heavily polluting vehicles are restricted from entering in order to lower air pollution. For example, from 2008 to 2009, Berlin's diesel particulate levels fell by a quarter after an LEZ was introduced. There are Europe-wide measures to conserve the shared atmosphere. These include limiting harmful emissions from the industry by using special filters or scrubbers in power station chimneys and encouraging the use of low-emission public transport, such as trams.

⬅ These trees in the Tatra Mountains, in Poland, have been badly damaged by air pollution. They have lost almost all their leaves because acid rain has poisoned the soil around them.

ICELAND

N

Scotland

Northern Ireland UNITED KINGDOM

North Sea

IRELAND

Wales

England NETHERLAND

London •

BELGIUM

Paris •

LUXEMBOURG

FRANCE

Alps

PORTUGAL

Pyrenees

SPAIN

ANDORRA

• **Madrid**

Corsic

Sardinia

Mediterranean Sea

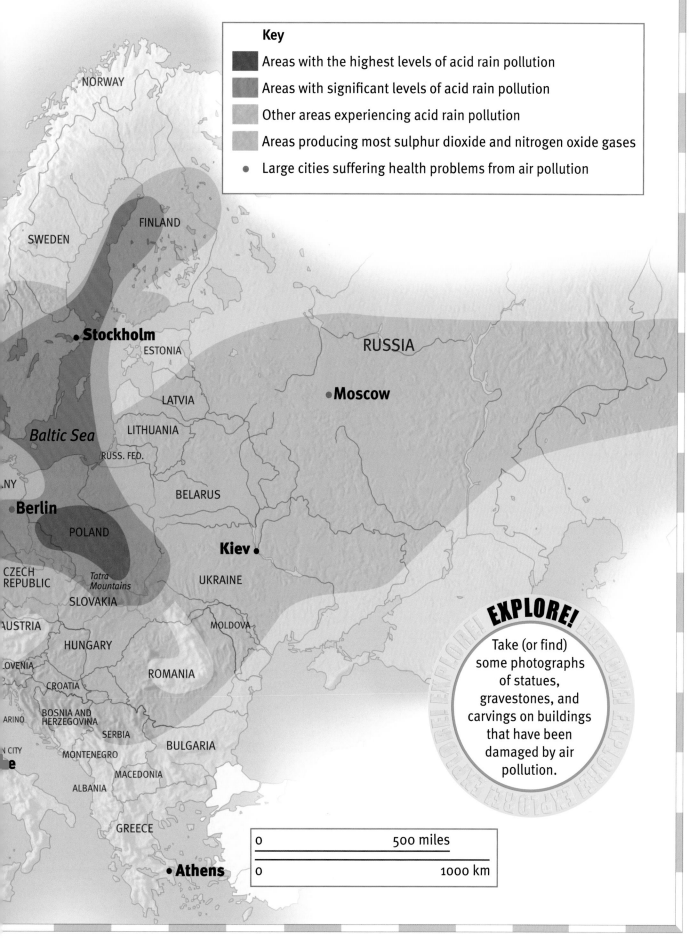

Key

- Areas with the highest levels of acid rain pollution
- Areas with significant levels of acid rain pollution
- Other areas experiencing acid rain pollution
- Areas producing most sulphur dioxide and nitrogen oxide gases
- Large cities suffering health problems from air pollution

NORWAY

FINLAND

SWEDEN

•Stockholm

ESTONIA

RUSSIA

LATVIA

•Moscow

LITHUANIA

Baltic Sea

RUSS. FED.

NY

BELARUS

Berlin

POLAND

Kiev •

CZECH
REPUBLIC

Tatra
Mountains

UKRAINE

SLOVAKIA

AUSTRIA

MOLDOVA

HUNGARY

OVENIA

ROMANIA

CROATIA

BOSNIA AND
HERZEGOVINA

ARINO

SERBIA

N CITY

MONTENEGRO

BULGARIA

e

MACEDONIA

ALBANIA

GREECE

•Athens

EXPLORE!

Take (or find)
some photographs
of statues,
gravestones, and
carvings on buildings
that have been
damaged by air
pollution.

0	500 miles
0	1000 km

The World: Climate Change

Climate is the normal pattern of weather in a place throughout the year. When climates change, they have widespread and significant effects on the natural world.

Scientists worldwide are noticing climate changes, including more frequent severe weather events, and warmer, drier, or wetter weather than usual every year. Climate change is ultimately caused by global warming. Greenhouse gases in the atmosphere trap heat from the Sun to keep the Earth at a certain temperature. This is called the greenhouse effect. However, burning fuels and other human activities adds more greenhouse gas, including carbon dioxide, to the atmosphere. This increases the greenhouse effect and causes global warming. Higher temperatures in some areas evaporate more water causing increased rain, or creating stronger winds. Sea levels are gradually rising because glaciers are melting. Warm seawater also takes up more space than cold seawater.

The map shows some of the effects of climate change worldwide. With continued global warming, scientists predict that many coastal settlements could become submerged. Already, some Pacific islands have been abandoned for this reason. People are trying to slow climate change by using solar and wind power instead of burning fossils fuels for energy. They are also adapting to climate change, for example by building hurricane-proof housing and flood defenses.

NORTH AMERICA

Atlantic Ocean

SOUTH AMERICA

Key: The effects of climate change

Extreme heat/drought
1 European heatwave 2003: 35,000 die in countries including France, Italy, and the Netherlands
2 African drought 2006: 17 million face food shortages in the Horn of Africa
3 Indonesian fires 1998: worst forest fires ever; 70 million people have health problems due to inhaling smoke

Extreme rain/wind
4 Pakistan floods 2010: 8 million people are homeless and 1,750 die
5 China landslides 2010: millions of people are affected when heavy rains cause landslides
6 Brazil hurricane 2004: the first ever recorded in the South Atlantic

Rising temperatures
7 Siberian permafrost: rising temperatures melt permafrost and release carbon into the air
8 Canadian polar bears: with less sea ice to catch seals, bear numbers drop and they must find food in towns

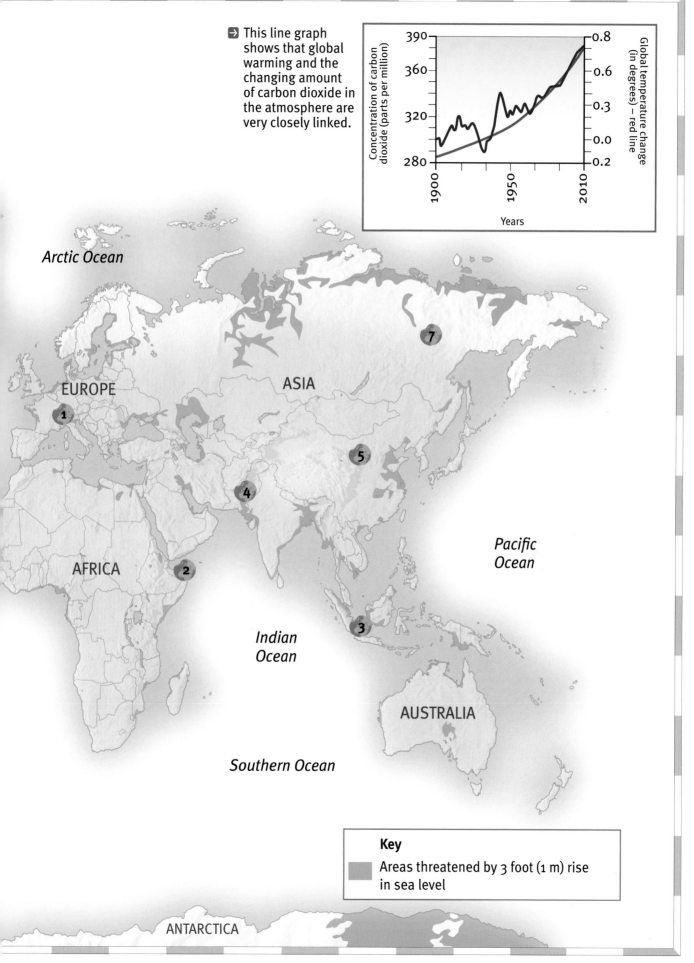

➡ This line graph shows that global warming and the changing amount of carbon dioxide in the atmosphere are very closely linked.

Concentration of carbon dioxide (parts per million)

Global temperature change (in degrees) – red line

Years

Arctic Ocean

EUROPE

ASIA

AFRICA

Pacific Ocean

Indian Ocean

AUSTRALIA

Southern Ocean

Key

Areas threatened by 3 foot (1 m) rise in sea level

ANTARCTICA

Now Test Yourself!

These questions will help you to revisit some of the information in this book. To answer the questions, you will need to use the table of contents at the beginning of the book and the index on p. 32, as well as the relevant pages on each topic.

1. Use the table of contents to find which pages show a map of:
(a) the forests in South America.
(b) wetland conservation in Europe.
(c) seas and oceans that have been overfished.

2. Use the index on p. 32 to find the pages that will tell you:
(a) which gases make up the Earth's atmosphere.
(b) what climate change is and what its causes are.

3. Use pp. 10-11 to find out which animal produces ivory and what this valuable material is made into.

4. Use pp. 14-15 to name the wetland in southern France which is famous for its wild horses and flamingos.

5. Use pp. 20-21 to find out how damage to coral reefs can be caused by:
(a) changes in the natural environment.
(b) the activities of people.

6. Name the natural features shown on this map: (A) desert, (B) island, (C) rain forest, (D) marine feature, (E) fishing area.

7. Use different pages in the book to pair these species with their correct natural habitats:
species: buffalo, giant panda, lichen, polyps.
habitats: bamboo forest, bare rock face, coral reef, grassland.

8. What are the main conservation reasons for having:
(a) reserves and armed rangers?
(b) Low Emission Zones?
(c) fishing quotas?
(d) IUCN Red List of Threatened Species?

Glossary

climate change (KLY-mut CHAYNJ)
Any long-term significant changes to the
weather pattern of a certain area. Climate
change can have natural causes, such as
volcano eruptions, and is also the result of
global warming.

conservation (kon-sur-VAY-shun) The care
of species and environments to ensure their
survival for future generations.

coral (KOR-ul) Underwater reefs made up of
limestone skeleton deposited by polyps.

deforestation (dee-for-uh-STAY-shun)
The loss of forest due to cutting down large
numbers of trees.

desertification (dih-zer-tih-fih-KAY-shun)
The word used to describe the spread of the
world's deserts.

drought (DROWT) A long period of time
with much less rainfall than usual.

ecosystem (EE-koh-sis-tem) A part of the
natural world, including the animals and
plants living in it.

environment (en-VY-ern-ment) The natural
environment is made up of hills, rivers,
lakes, and wildlife; the human environment
includes buildings and roads.

erosion (ih-ROH-zhun) The wearing away
of the land surface by wind and water.

extinction (ek-STINGK-shun) What happens
when the very last member of a species dies.

global warming (GLOH-bul WAWRM-ing)
Rising temperatures worldwide, caused by
the increase of gases in the air that trap the
Sun's heat near Earth.

greenhouse effect (GREEN-hows eh-FEKT)
The warming effect on the atmosphere of
burning fossil fuels. This is one cause of
global warming.

heritage (HER-uh-tij) Valuable human and
natural features inherited from the past.

irrigation (ih-rih-GAY-shun) The carrying
of water to farming land through ditches
or pipes.

migration (my-GRAY-shun) The seasonal
movement of wildlife in search of food
throughout the year.

national park (NASH-nul PARK) Land that
is set aside by a country's government for
people to visit and animals to live on.

pollution (puh-LOO-shun) Damage to the
environment caused by harmful substances.

species (SPEE-sheez) A single kind of living
thing. All people are one species.

wetlands (WET-landz) Areas where soil is
permanently saturated with water.

Index

Websites

Due to the changing nature of Internet links, PowerKids Press has developed an online list of websites related to the subject of this book. This site is updated regularly. Please use this link to access the list:
www.powerkidslinks.com/mew/cons/